SWIMMING TECHNIQUES IN PICTURES

If you were taught to swim by the sink-or-swim method, or just "picked it up," chances are you are not swimming correctly. You may be able to get from one end of the pool to the other, but you expend too much energy and find yourself tiring quickly. For some reason, swimming is just not the enjoyable sport you feel it could be. Why not take the time to break bad swimming habits and learn new ones — habits that will assure that you get all of the recreation, healthy exercise, and fun out of swimming that the sport can provide?

If you *can't* swim now, Bob Horn, head coach of the UCLA swimming team, will teach you how. With the help of two expert swimmers — Diana Dann and Russell Webb — and sequenced surface and underwater photography, Coach Horn illustrates and explains clearly and precisely each motion and movement that goes into the four major swimming strokes: crawl, backstroke, breaststroke, and butterfly. Breath control, dives, exercises, treading water, competitive swimming, and water survival are also fully described and illustrated. *Swimming Techniques in Pictures* is an important instruction manual for swimmers and would-be swimmers of all ages.

SWIMMING TECHNIQUES IN PICTURES

Expert Instruction by UCLA Swimming Coach

BOB HORN

Underwater sequences and still photographs by

J. BARRY HERRON of Globe Photos

GROSSET & DUNLAP

Publishers   New York

We wish to thank the Amateur Athletic Union of the United States for their permission to reprint portions of their *Official Swimming Rules,* and to acknowledge the guidance and help of Harry Hainsworth and H. Lynn Jamison of the AAU in the writing of the chapter on Competitive Swimming.

To James R. Smith, the grandfather of American water polo and swimming, without whose guidance and dedication none of this would have been possible.

CONTENTS

PREFACE

Swimming is simply the physical adjustment your body makes to the environment of water. Although three-fourths of our planet is water, evolution has seen fit to limit man to operate most freely in an envelope of air. But man's ingenuity has devised a system of techniques, using the water itself and a coordinated use of lung and muscle power, to render himself fairly comfortable, if not completely at home, in the ocean, in a lake, or in a swimming pool. The photographs and the text that follow are a close and clear examination of the techniques that allow man to survive in, and enjoy, this alien world.

BREATHING

Breath control is basic for the beginning, intermediate, or more advanced swimmer. And the constant practice of breath control is fundamental to perfecting the execution of the four swimming strokes that will be examined in this book: the crawl, the backstroke, the breaststroke, and the butterfly.

The exercise shown in the following sequence of photographs, essential for someone who is just learning how to swim, is just as beneficial for the swimmer who may not be breathing efficiently.

As the swimmer stands (1) in shallow water, his right hand grips the gutter lip of the pool wall. His head is held erect. Holding the head in this way stabilizes the swimmer and prevents water from rushing up his nose.

A normal-size breath is taken, not a deep one. Then the swimmer lowers himself (2) into the water, keeping his head erect (3–5). As his nose nears the surface of the water, the swimmer begins to expel his intake of air through his nose, causing ripples in the water. He continues to expel air (3–10), even as he has submerged and surfaced completely.

Now you are the swimmer and you are trying this yourself. Once you are under the water and expelling air through your nose, you are apt to be aware of an uncomfortable pressure. This is the result of your exhalation of air beneath the water. This is a feeling you must get used to. It is quite different from the sensation of breathing out above the surface of the water without having to think about it. Apart from the fact that the latter is a reflex action while the former is a reflex being developed, an entirely different medium is involved — water. In this environment, air must be forced from the nose. Not all of the air inhaled should be expelled, however. That

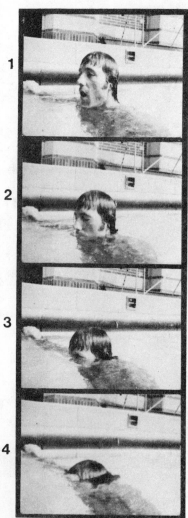

Breathing (above water)

With Russell Webb looking on, Coach Bob Horn demonstrates how to begin breathing exercises — by taking a normal-size breath.

Expelling air underwater causes an uncomfortable feeling of pressure which one must get used to.

would result in a loss of buoyancy. Your lungs are an inflatable source, a sort of built-in inner tube. Retaining some air holds your body close to the surface.

Controlled exhalation accomplishes two things: water is prevented from rushing up your nose; and enough air is retained so that you don't find yourself gasping for breath when you reach the surface.

Instead, when you break through the water, "blast out" that residual air through your nose *and* mouth. This forceful expelling of air can be seen clearly in 8 and 9 of the above-water photograph sequence.

As you blast out, it is most important to release *all* the air you are holding. Most people worry about taking in air at this point. It is a natural response. They are afraid of releasing the air they have kept in reserve for fear they might not get that fresh intake. But a new habit must be learned. Once you are used to the feeling of blasting out your reserve air and following it with a normal intake (10), you are on your way. Whatever you do, avoid deep-breath intakes. Storing up larger and larger amounts of air can only lead to fatigue and poor use of oxygen.

The amount of time spent underwater in this exercise should be greater than your brief visits to the surface. For every six seconds spent under the water slowly expelling your air intake, only two seconds should be spent above the surface blasting out your air reserve and taking in your normal breath. And that is at the beginning. As you become more proficient, the length of time out of water should be shortened and the ratio to the time spent underwater will be altered.

Why bother with keeping your head under at all? Because swimming with it above the water is not terribly effective. Any part of the body that remains out of the water is offering resistance to your movement through the water, and you expend more energy than necessary to get where you want to go. That is why you tire quickly and find yourself out of breath after only a short swim.

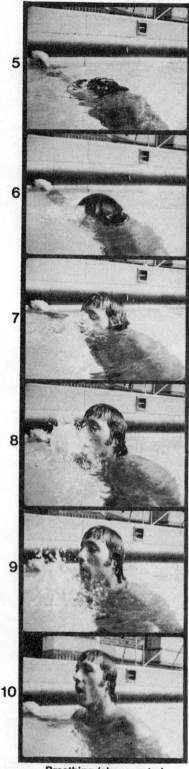

5

6

7

8

9

10

Breathing (above water)

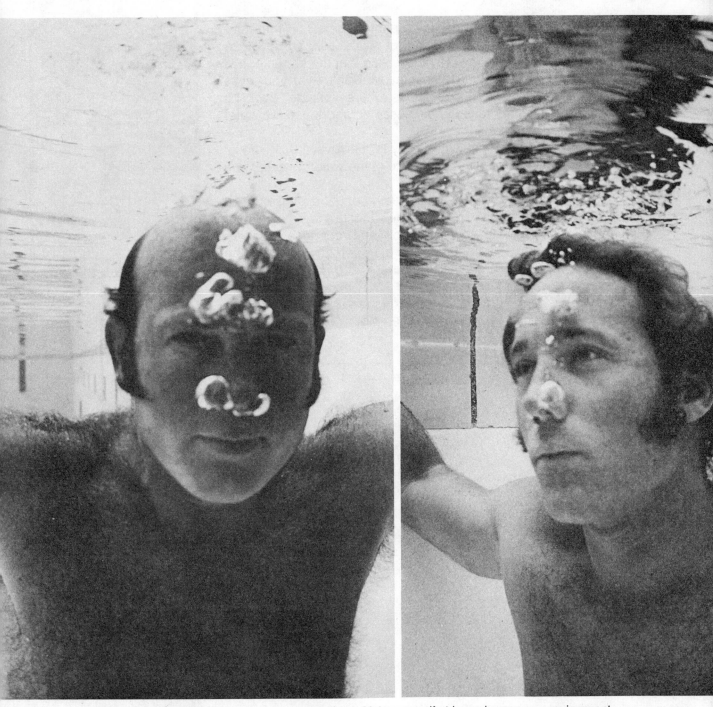

Once underwater, open your eyes and use them. Make yourself at home in your new environment.

In the sequence of underwater photographs (1–6) for this breathing exercise, notice the stream of air bubbles produced by the expelled air. It is also important to notice that the swimmer has his eyes open for balance and orientation. Don't keep your eyes closed underwater. Don't try to guess where you are. Look for object relationships; try to judge distances; in short, use the water as your new environment.

There *is* a time for shutting the eyes, however (3). It should occur the moment you break the surface of the water, whether you are going under or coming up.

Once you feel at ease with this breath-control exercise, move into the deeper end of the pool where the water is a few inches over your head. With your feet touching bottom and your nose underwater expelling air, push up from the balls of your feet. Bob out of the water, blasting out your air; then breathe in and drop back to the bottom. Expel your air and push up and out of the water again. This bobbing in the deep end is a very relaxing breathing exercise and one that experienced swimmers often employ.

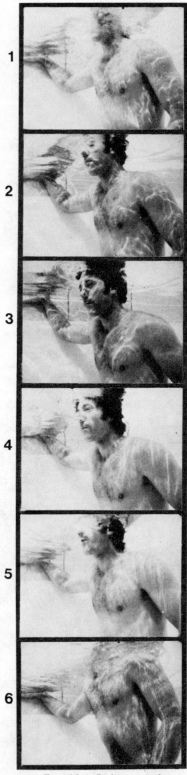

Breathing (below water)

THE CRAWL

1 Push-off and Glide

Push-off and glide establishes the body position and provides the body with momentum before the stroke has begun.

To do this, the swimmer stands with his back to the wall in the shallow end of the pool (1). One foot rests on the pool floor. One leg, usually the right, is bent, and the foot is placed flat against the wall.

Then the swimmer extends her hands and arms in front and lowers her head to the water's surface (2). The hands should remain about six inches apart, or close enough to produce a narrowing of the shoulders and a more streamlined contour to the whole body. The palms are facing down. Once the head is down in the water, it becomes a part of the contour; buoyancy is automatic.

At this point, the foot that has been resting on the pool floor is lifted and joins the other foot resting against the pool wall (3). Now both feet appear to be fairly near the surface as they rest against the wall. Because the head is providing buoyancy, the swimmer does not sink in this position. It is time now to push off with the feet (4 and 5).

Getting the head in the water for that buoyancy before the push-off is very important. A common tendency is to thrust forward with the head out of the water, with the result that the body pushes out and up from the water — just what must be avoided. Remember, any part of the body out of the water merely offers resistance and wastes energy; resistance retards forward momentum, and that momentum is vital. Swimming is very much like trying to push a stalled car. It is very hard to get going, but once it starts rolling forward, the pushing gets easier. In swimming, anything that creates a negative force — for example, keeping your head out of water — is like trying to push that car uphill.

Push-off and Glide (above water)

With the head in the water in preparation for the push-off, buoyancy is automatic.

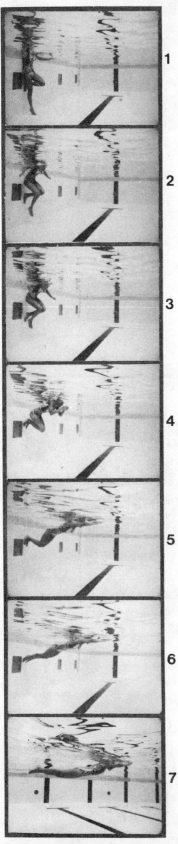

Push-off and Glide (below water)

The underwater sequence of photographs (1–7) clearly shows the position of the feet. It also shows the arms before they move out in front. They should be resting against the wall to keep the legs and feet in the proper position until the last moment. Any drifting from this position at the wall will weaken the leverage provided by the legs in the push-off.

As the head reaches the underwater position in 4, both feet are drawn up against the wall. Now they wait for the hands to extend out in front (5). The feet should not push off until the head and hands are in their proper underwater position. If the hands are extended *after* the push-off, a negative force is created by the arms moving forward through the water and the force of the forward thrust will be reduced.

After the feet leave the wall (6) the swimmer is into the glide (7). This is the taking-off point for the stroke itself.

Bracing yourself to the wall of the pool in this manner allows you to isolate and practice your kick.

On the downstroke, the leg pushes at the water in a power thrust.

Kicking from the Wall

The movement of the legs in the stroke is best learned and perfected by isolating that movement and performing it in a stationary position at the wall.

The body is supported in the water with the arms and hands (1). The left hand grips the gutter lip while the right hand and arm are underwater. The right arm is held at about a 45-degree angle with the palm of the hand flat against the wall. The arms, in effect, create a kind of bracket, holding the body up and making it independent of any other action for support. This frees the legs to do their work properly and keeps them in the position in which they will function during the stroke.

The downstroke of the left leg (1–5) is generated from the hip. The leg, in effect, becomes the stick of a pendulum that is hinged in two places — at the knee and at the ankle. On this downward stroke, avoid the common error of bending the knee too much. It should be bent just enough to force the hinged movement of the ankle that follows. The knee is the leader in this action. The ankle is the follower. At the bottom end of the downstroke (5) the ankle is lower in the water than the knee. The ankle must be very relaxed and loose so that the water pressure on the downstroke of the leg will bring the toes to a point, as in 5.

The upstroke of the leg (5–7) is also generated at the hip; it commences even as the toes of the foot are in their pointed position at the bottom of the downstroke. As the knee comes into play again and bends once more, the ankle is snapped back. Now the toes point straight down to the floor of the pool and the foot is no longer in an extended position; the heel has reached the water surface (7).

The foot actually makes a small circle in its travels, moving away on the downstroke to the far side of the diameter and returning on the upstroke to the near side.

The most efficient part of the kick comes in the downstroke, when the leg can bend at the knee and push at the water. On the upstroke, when there is no bending at the knee, this thrust is lessened.

Riding on this power thrust from one leg, the other leg has recovered and now begins its downstroke action (6 and 7).

The kick in the crawl is minimized in distance swimming because it is not as efficient as the arms.

Kicking (below water)

The Armstroke

Beginning with an underwater view (1–7), we see the left arm in the power phase of the stroke, while the right arm is recovering above the water. As the left arm pulls through the water and down toward the pool floor (1–3), the elbow is slightly bent. When it reaches its vertical position (at a 90-degree angle with the surface), it is neither out at the side nor adjacent to the body, but is at a point that would touch the center of the body line (4). If an imaginary pane of glass dropped vertically toward the pool floor from the center of the body, the hand (at the end of the "pull" cycle) would be grazing that pane of glass on one side. Similarly, when the right hand reaches the bottom of its pull in the water, it touches the other side of that imagined glass pane. If both hands were to operate in the pull simultaneously, they would seem to come close to meeting at a point vertical to the midsection of the body. This hand position can be seen clearly in 4.

What is probably the most important part of the armstroke begins with the push phase (4). This is the strongest element of the stroke. Since the water causes a good deal of resistance at this point, a common error is to let the arm slide sideways and come out of the water too early for recovery. This push cycle follow-through is shown clearly in 6 and 7.

In the above-water sequence, the right arm at the end of the push cycle is beginning its recovery (1). The first portion of the arm that recovers is the elbow. The hand should not be at a level above the elbow at this point. In 2 we can see the relationship between the hand and the elbow at the start of recovery. The position of the hand here is parallel to the forearm. The wrist, at this point, should

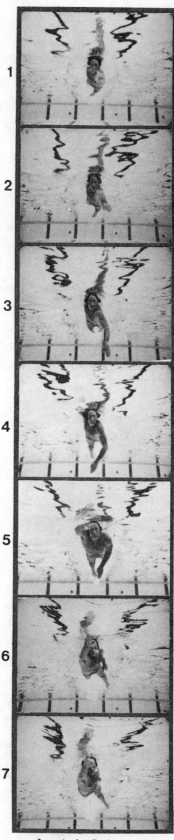

Armstroke (below water)

not be bent. The hand is not cupped, but relaxed. The fingers are fairly close together, neither spread nor touching (3 and 4).

On the reentry of the hand into the water (5 and 6), the elbow is still above the hand-level. The arm should feel as though you were reaching over a small barrel floating in your way. The fingertips enter the water first, not the palm or any part of the arm. The hand is then extended to the catch position, a point that is four to six inches below the surface of the water. At this point, both the hand and the arm are in the water (1).

The catch position initiates the power phase of the arm underwater, as was described earlier. Now the pull begins again, changing to the push cycle after the arm reaches its vertical position. With the completion of the push (just before recovery), the hand is virtually adjacent to the thigh before leaving the water.

These, then, are the two phases of the armstroke: the pull literally pulls the body through the water; the push, which begins after the arm reaches its vertical position, literally pushes the body farther on.

With regard to the entry of the hand into the water, the hand is at the distance point from the head most comfortable for the individual swimmer. What he or she must remember to do is to reach over that barrel and go for the catch position.

In the armstroke, finally, the shoulders roll from side to side while the head is held straight and still. The head is used as a kind of pivot that creates a line of axis down through your body. The right shoulder on the power phase of the right arm should be down in the water and the left shoulder will be up and out of the water for the recovery phase of the left arm. The shoulders are never locked flat on the surface of the water.

Armstroke (above water)

A kickboard is perfect for practicing the kick away from the pool wall.

The fingertips enter the water first as you reach "over the barrel" for the catch position.
The pull cycle begins from this catch position.

¹ Breathing in Stroke

In sequence 1 through 9 the swimmer is breathing on his left side. One side is usually preferred and therefore remains constant. Making the catch with his right arm (1), the left arm is in the power phase, at its vertical position. The head is still held straight. The head begins to pivot with the shoulder (2) as he approaches the end of his push cycle in the power phase of the left arm underwater. His face starts to clear the water (3), which is pushed aside. In the water, a kind of bow wave is formed off the swimmer's forehead, created by the pushing action. Right behind that bow wave is a small trough of air. The face can then be turned into that trough and the breath taken without having to turn the head around completely and out of the water, thereby throwing off the body axis. As seen in 4, the waterline on the forehead should be just above the eyes and below the hairline.

The bow wave and trough will vary according to the speed that you move through the water. In the case of the beginner who may move slowly, the trough will be shallow and the swimmer will have to roll further in the shoulder to bring the head, still fixed in position, around for air. With a more advanced, faster swimmer, the trough is deeper, the bow wave greater, and the body is riding higher in the water, so the shoulder and head roll will be less.

As he blasts out his residual air, the water flies away from the swimmer's mouth (4 and 5), much the same as it did in the bobbing and breathing exercise. The swimmer takes a breath (6 and 7). Then the head is turned and is just under the arm, making its recovery out of the water (8 and 9). This is the advanced stage of the breath cycle and the timing here is critical. Exhalation and intake of air is accomplished rapidly and the head returns to its position in the water (1), thus stabilizing the body.

(For the purpose of these illustrations, the breathing cycle was slowed down by the swimmer to accommodate the photographer. The swimmer is, therefore, taking a longer time to go through the cycle than he normally would in a competitive situation.)

Also, for the beginning swimmer the breathing cycle would begin much earlier, when the arm was back at the leg just before making its recovery out of the water. With the arm still in the water, there is more buoyancy and the body is higher in the water, putting the head in a better breathing position. With the arm out of the water, some buoyancy is lost and the body rides lower. If you take a long time to breathe — you should determine this during your breathing exercises — you should begin the breath cycle at a very

Breathing in Stroke

A breath is taken from the trough behind the swimmer's own bow wave.

With the advanced swimmer, the "roll" is minimized so that the swimmer's forehead is on the bow wave and he can look forward.

Breathing in Stroke

8

9

early stage. If you breathe on the right, this would occur when the left arm is in the underwater pulling cycle of the power phase. At the follow-through stage, with the arm back at the leg, you are rolling further, getting your air, and starting to put your head back in the water as the arm comes out to make its recovery. With the more experienced swimmer, the arm has almost entered the water while the head still has not returned to it (8 and 9). The speed of the advanced swimmer, the depth of his air trough, and the fact that his body rides higher in the water, enable him to take his breath at a much later stage (as demonstrated in the photo sequence). With the beginning swimmer who takes his breath somewhat earlier, the roll of the shoulder will be greater and the head will turn slightly so that the face will have turned nearly 180 degrees. This movement will also be accompanied by a slight roll in the hip.

Ideally, in the advanced stages of swimming you want to rest your face on the bow wave and actually look forward slightly. The intermediate or beginning swimmer is more apt to be looking back or skyward because the head is turned so far. The resting of the face on the bow wave can be seen in 5.

Turn, Push-off, and Glide

1

2

3

Once again the wall is used. Above water, in 1, the swimmer's right arm recovers and he reaches for the wall with it (2). At that point, his left arm should remain back against his left thigh. In this grab turn, the swimmer takes hold of the wall with his right hand (3). His head remains down until he makes contact with the wall and his body is in a glide phase. His legs have begun to drop toward the pool floor and the head is starting to come out of the water (4). The body should be kept low. When it is in a vertical position (5), the trailing arm back at the thigh (in this case the left) drops below the surface. This helps him to get his head and shoulders below the surface prior to the push-off.

4

5

Turn, Push-off, and Glide (above water)

In 6 the head is vertical and out of the water so that breath can be taken.

With the feet now up against the wall (7), the left arm is perpendicular to the water's surface. Now the left arm moves to assist the head and shoulders in their return to the water to a depth of six inches or so (8 to 10). At this point, the right arm begins to make a recovery and entry on the armstroke.

The push-off with the feet is not done until the head and shoulder have returned to the water and the arms are extended in front for the glide that precedes the stroke (11).

On this turn you actually push off on your side. It is in the glide phase that you roll back on your stomach (12) and return the body to the surface. You begin your kick after this leveling off, since the wall is now a few feet behind you, and then go immediately into your armstroke. The armstroke is begun with the arm opposite your breathing arm. If you breathe on your right, begin with your left arm. The start of the stroke should coincide with your return to the surface in the glide.

Turn, Push-off, and Glide (above water)

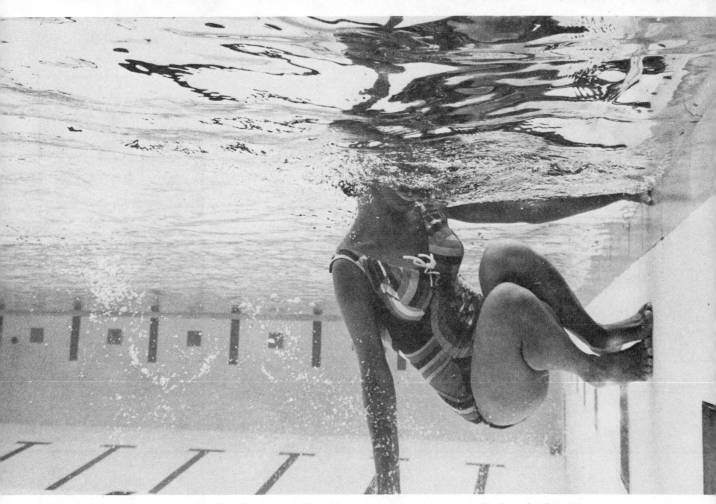

In the grab turn, hold your push-off until your head is underwater and your arms are in place for the glide.

Below the surface, the swimmer's legs are planted on the wall (1). Note that the trailing (left) arm is now vertical. In 2 it is helping to get the swimmer's head and shoulder back in the water. The arm is actually pushing the water up, which, in turn, forces the body down. Photo 3 shows the reentry of the hand that has left the wall. Ready to push off (4), the hands are together, the head is submerged, the feet are on the wall, and the knees are bent. The head is underwater about six or eight inches (5). Arms and hands are stretched forward (6) as he begins the push-off. Photo 7 shows that he is in the glide phase.

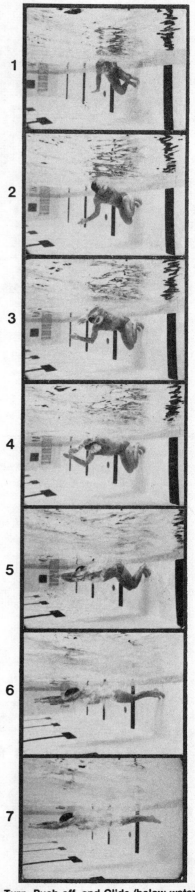

Turn, Push-off, and Glide (below water)

THE BACKSTROKE

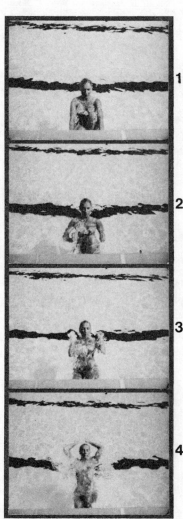

Push-off and Glide (above water)

Push-off and Glide

1 Above water, the swimmer faces the wall (1) and holds on to the gutter lip with both hands. The legs are in a bent and raised position. They are off the pool floor and the feet are planted against the wall. The head is held erect. In the below-water sequence (1), one leg is raised slightly higher than the other; in this case, the left leg. This helps maintain contact with the wall and prepares for a strong and balanced push-off.

2 In this position, a beginner is likely to make the common error of simply "sitting" in the water with a rounded back, making the hips drop and giving the body a "U" shape. Then, in the thrust of the push-off, the back offers resistance to the water and forces the head out of the water. Once away from the wall and with the loss of momentum, the head drops back into the water and water rushes uncomfortably up the nose. It is important to avoid this experience, **3** for this kind of discomfort can easily discourage the novice who is not so much interested in forward progress as in keeping that water from causing problems in breathing.

Since the proper body position in the push-off is critical, assistance in positioning is advisable. First, the head should be angled back toward the water so that the body will be almost level when it enters the water. As in the crawl, if the head is up the feet or the **4** hips will drop. It is thus helpful to aid the swimmer in putting the back of the head on the water surface and demonstrating that the head will find buoyant support. In this position (6), the swimmer must get the feeling of the waterline on the head and face. He or

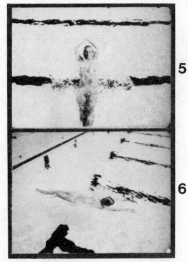

Push-off and Glide (above water)

Push-off and Glide (below water)

she must also sense that the back is flat against the surface and that the hips are raised and are likewise at the surface.

Once this head position is learned, the push-off from the wall is the next step. The first movement is a releasing of the hands from the wall (2). Now the hands, with palms up and thumbs touching the sides of the body, move up toward the head and remain at or just below the surface of the water (3). The arms, too, should remain at the surface of the water or just slightly below it. Then the hands are extended beyond the head and remain in the water. If they are allowed to rise out of the water, the head will drop.

The thrust back with the legs should be a measured and controlled movement, not a forceful one. If there is too much thrust, water has a tendency to rush over the head and face because suction is created, pulling the water up and over the face at the end of the power thrust. So the momentum of the thrust should be fast enough to provide forward progress yet slow enough to avoid this suction effect. Pushing off in the crawl doesn't require this controlled thrust since the face is already in the water.

Now, with the feet away from the wall and the arms and hands extended straight back behind the head, the swimmer is in the glide position (6) and ready to begin the kick.

Swimmer Diana Dann demonstrates how *not* to push off if you are a beginner. This method is acceptable, however, for a proficient swimmer.

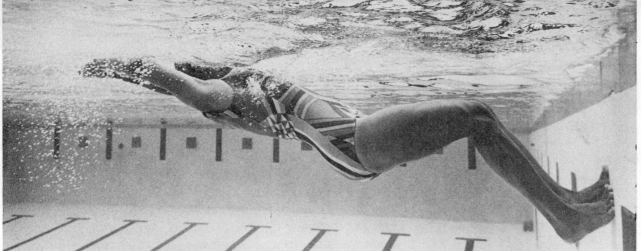

The thrust of the backstroke push-off should be measured and controlled for the beginner.

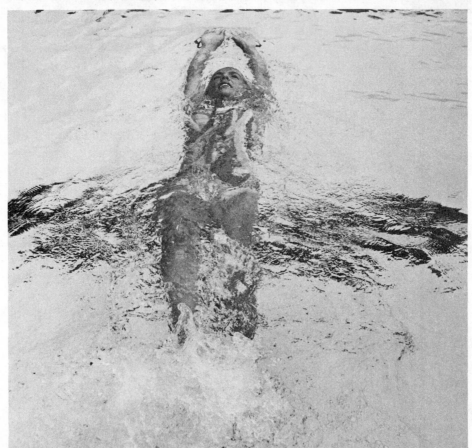

In the naturally buoyant glide position, the shallow backstroke kick alone is enough to propel a swimmer through the water.

If the ankle is properly relaxed, the pressure of the water will cause a foot in the power phase (rising) to point.

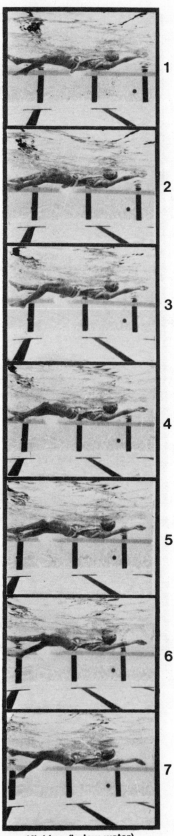

Kicking (below water)

1 The Kick

This is much the same kick as that performed in the crawl, with these differences: the swimmer is now lying on his back and the depth of the kick will be shallower.

The main power phase of the kick will come on the upsweep of the leg. (In the crawl it came on the downsweep.) In 1 the left leg is seen at the end of the stroke with the toe of the left foot reaching the surface. Simultaneously, the leg from the hip to the knee has already begun its downward motion toward recovery. It will pull the bottom part of the leg down after it, straightening out the full length of the limb, with the heel leading the foot and pointing toward the bottom of the pool. The toes more or less point toward the surface. This is the least efficient part of the kick.

As the foot reaches the bottom of the recovery, the pendulum action takes over and the leg, from hip to knee, pushes up toward the surface. As this upward thrust begins in the power phase, the pressure of the water acts upon the foot; with the ankle properly relaxed the foot will extend and the toes will point forward. This is where the foot makes its catch in the water and pushes it away from the body, thus providing the required forward motion.

As the legs operate alternately (one in power phase, one in recovery), the knees should pass each other and achieve a vertical distance between them of between two to four inches (4).

From knee to foot, the leg (5) extends toward the surface and reaches the conclusion of its power phase. By 7 the top half of the left leg is moving into its recovery stage, while the other leg has brought the right foot into the catch position of the power phase.

The Armstroke

The catch of the right arm at the start of its power phase is seen from above (1). The arm should enter the water at a slight angle away from the body. If it enters straight back from the shoulder, its pull through the water will propel the body sideways.

The hand should enter the water with the little finger leading and the palm facing outward. At a point four to six inches below the surface, the hand reaches its catch. The hand should remain at this depth through the power phase. If it dips lower into the water, it has a tendency to push the body up and out of the water, thus sacrificing buoyancy. Then, at the bottom of the power phase, it will push water up, pulling the body even further down after its loss of buoyancy. Neither a sideways motion nor having the body rise and fall in the water is desirable. The swimmer should remain stable in the water with his waterline remaining fairly constant. Like a row-boat, the swimmer's body should ride the water with his arms, acting like oars, providing the forward movement.

During this power phase of the arm, the angle of the wrist changes, as it does in the crawl. In the pull cycle — or until the arm reaches the shoulder line — the hand remains straight on extension of the arm. As it goes into its push cycle, the hand bends back at the wrist to push the water in a direction opposite to the body's forward motion.

Photo 2 shows the beginning of the power phase in the right arm (the pull cycle). The left arm has completed its power phase and is beginning its recovery at the hip. As the right arm goes into its push cycle of the power phase, the left arm is out of the water and in its recovery stage (4 and 5).

In the recovery stage, the left arm moves up and out of the water with the arm extended and the hand straight up, palm facing inward. This movement is facilitated with a roll of the left shoulder slightly out of the water. The right shoulder, meanwhile, is rolling slightly under, assisting the right arm in its power phase.

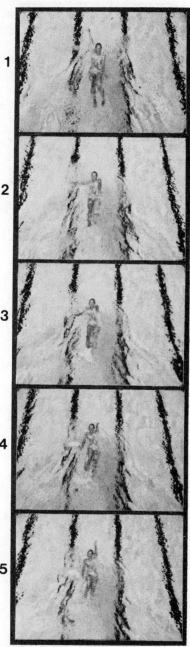

Armstroke (above water)

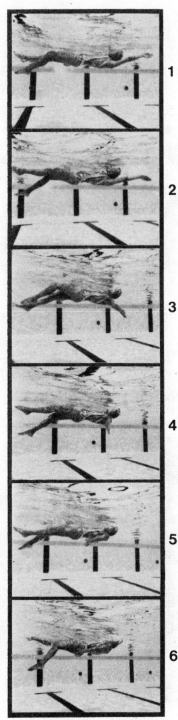

Armstroke (below water)

The arm will reach a vertical position; as it passes beyond this position and moves back down behind the head toward its catch in the water, the wrist will turn the hand so that the palm will now face outward. With the elbow leading the arm's descent, the little finger will be in position to break the surface for the catch. Now the left shoulder will roll down into the water to assist the power phase of the left arm, while the right shoulder will roll out of the water to bring the right arm to recovery.

Throughout the alternating power phase and recovery of the arms, the head should be back in the water (as in the push-off and glide) and the chin down toward the chest, always motionless. This will provide stability for the rest of the body, with the head acting as a kind of gyroscope.

As seen from underwater (1), the left arm is making the catch. In this particular sequence, the pull cycle being performed is most commonly used by an intermediate swimmer since it is a straight-arm pull and easy to coordinate. With a more advanced swimmer, the pull cycle would show more elbow bend and the arm would be seen closer to the surface. This latter technique brings the hand closer to the body and results in more stroke power. The arm is foreshortened and there is more strength in it. It is true that in this procedure, with the loss of the straight arm, leverage is sacrificed. But with the bend of the elbow, force and speed are acquired. In employing this technique it is important that the hand not be allowed (while it is operating so close to the surface) to break through the surface. This will result in a trapping of air, called cavitation, and the swimmer will lose control in the water.

In 2 the left arm is shown in the beginning of the pull cycle. In 3 the pull is at the maximum depth and the arm is pulling parallel to the surface. The left shoulder is down in the water assisting the left arm in the power phase. The right shoulder is above water assisting the right arm in recovery. Photo 4 shows the beginning of the push cycle for the left arm. At 5 it has reached the end of this cycle; and at 6 the arm is down at the thigh, ready for recovery.

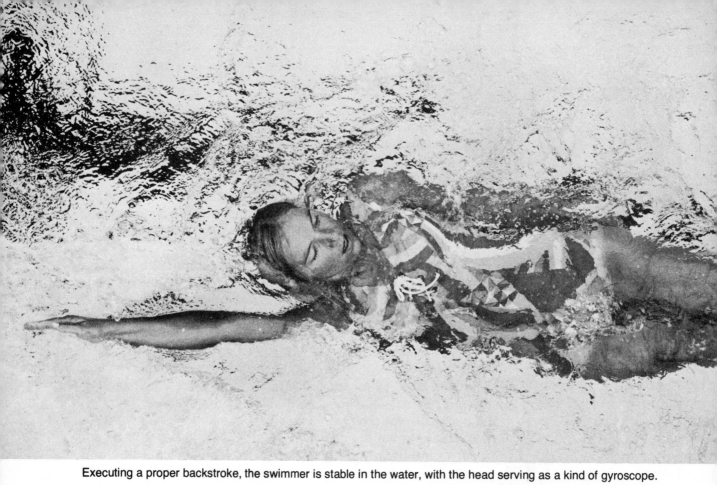

Executing a proper backstroke, the swimmer is stable in the water, with the head serving as a kind of gyroscope.

After the turn, the arm at the end of the power phase should still extend toward the opposite end of the pool.

Turn, Push-off, and Glide

In 1 the right arm is extending toward the wall in the catch of the armstroke. Instead of completing its power phase, the right hand takes hold of the gutter lip and pivots the body sideways in the water. If the arm has not reached the wall when it makes its catch, the legs should continue the kick until it does.

In 2 and 3 the legs begin to drop and the knees bend. At 4 the body has reached a vertical position and the head is out of the water but close to the wall until the vertical position is fully achieved.

The left arm has remained in its position at the end of its power phase and is still extended underwater toward the opposite end of the pool. Here, as in 5, it is assisting the swimmer in maintaining his balance. The feet are now planted against the wall. In 6 the right arm leaves the wall and is extended and placed behind the head with the left arm. The head drops slightly underwater. Breath control now plays an important role. Because of the momentum of the push-off, the head will forcefully break through the surface, creating a bow wave. If the swimmer is correctly expelling his air intake at a controlled rate, no water will rush up the nose.

Again, as in the crawl, the push-off with the legs is not executed until the arms and the head are in the water in their proper positions, where no resistance will be encountered. With the arms extended beyond the head, the push-off is executed (7 and 8). Now the body is in the glide position; as the feet leave the wall, the kick begins, followed by the armstroke.

From the glide, the right arm begins its power phase underwater, while the left arm remains in its glide position until the right arm has completed its power phase and is approaching recovery. Then the left arm moves into its power phase underwater as the right arm recovers.

Turn, Push-off, and Glide (below water)

THE BREASTSTROKE

The push-off and glide in the breaststroke and the butterfly are identical with those in the crawl, since all three strokes are executed with the body facing down in the water.

However, the breaststroke and the butterfly are quite different from the crawl and the backstroke, where the arm and legs operate alternately. In the breaststroke and the butterfly, the legs perform their power phases and recoveries simultaneously, with the arms doing the same.

The Kick

To learn this kick, the swimmer holds on to the wall in the same way he or she did in learning the kick for the crawl. As seen from the top and above the water in 1, the legs are together, the feet extended, and the toes pointed. Photo 2 shows the beginning of the recovery. The movement of the legs during recovery should be slower and more subtle in execution than in the kick. This is because the leg movement during recovery is creating an essentially negative force in the water. That negative force is somewhat ameliorated if the water turbulence created by the legs during recovery is kept at a minimum. At 3 the legs have bent at the knee and the feet have

1

2

3

Kicking (above water)

In the breaststroke, the arms and legs perform simultaneously.

come toward the surface, heels first, in a very narrow fashion. In 4 the legs have reached maximum recovery; while the knees have remained close together, the feet have moved apart. The toes have turned out and now the legs are prepared for the power phase of the kick.

The kick is executed close to the surface, but the feet should not break the water. This would create a pocket of air, or a cavitation effect, and some control in the water would be lost. Thrusting from the hips, the thighs push the legs more or less straight back. The feet move outward in a small circular motion and the water is pushed aside with the insides of the feet and the legs (up to the knees). This action can be seen in 5 and 6, where the legs are nearing the end of the power stroke. Photo 7 shows the full extension of the legs, still slightly apart. But by 8 the heels have come together and the toes are pointed. Now the body has reached the glide phase of the kick.

The power phase of the kick is sometimes described as a snapping of the legs and the feet back into the glide. The glide phase is extremely important in the breaststroke. It must be taken after the power phase of the kick; the reasons for this will become clearer when the mechanics of the total stroke are examined at a later stage.

4

5

6

7

8

Kicking (above water)

Braced to the pool wall, practice keeping water resistance during the kick recovery at a minimum.

The kick, as seen from under the water and behind the swimmer, is shown in 1, as the swimmer holds on to the wall. The legs are fully extended along with the feet and the toes are pointed. In 2 the legs have begun their recovery. They are bending at the knees and are still together. At the top of the recovery (3), the knees have moved about two to three inches apart and the legs are approaching the catch. The heels are still close together, but the toes are starting to spread. In 4 the legs are at maximum catch and the narrowness of the kick can be seen. In photo 5 the power phase of the kick begins with the circular motion of the feet as they move apart and beyond the line of the knees. Photo 6 shows the end of the power phase. The feet are moving back together and the water is being pushed away by the insides of the lower legs and the feet. In 7 the ankles snap back and the feet move toward each other. In 8 (as in 1) the feet are back together with the legs. The toes are pointed. The body is in glide.

Years ago, the Red Cross swimming manuals called this the frog kick; it was a much wider kick than that demonstrated here. The recovery had a great deal of negative resistance connected with it, since it was neither slowly nor subtly executed. This new style of kicking, which is far more efficient, is referred to as the whip kick. It is a narrow kick. The feet at their widest position should not go beyond the width of the shoulders.

Kicking (below water, rear view)

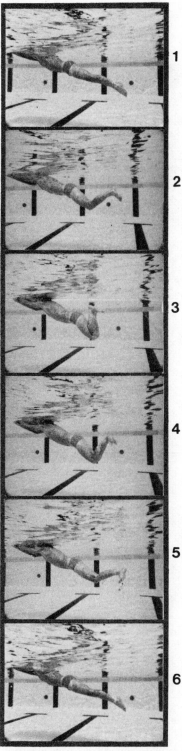

1

2

3

4

5

6

Kicking (below water, side view)

Another important phase of the kick can best be examined from a side view. In this sequence, the kick is executed with the aid of a kickboard. This enables the swimmer — freed from his concentration on the armstroke — to get a better feeling for the kick itself.

Photo 1 shows the full extension of the legs with toes pointed and body in the glide phase. Photo 2 marks the beginning of the recovery. The legs are bending, but the primary bend is from the knees and not the hips. A common error is to draw up at the waist so the legs (from the hips to the knees) will drop into a vertical position. This is a poor technique and not desirable. The body should remain fairly straight from the hips to the knees; the major portion of the bend in recovery is only from the knees. In 3 the legs have completely recovered; they are at a 90-degree angle to the surface. The heels are very near the surface — about an inch or two below — and the toes, at this point, spread for the catch; in 4 the backward thrust can be seen. The power phase nearing its conclusion is shown in 5. In 6 the ankles have snapped back, the toes are pointed, and the body is in the glide phase.

With the legs at full recovery, the heels should be close to but not break the water's surface.

Armstroke (below water)

1 The Armstroke

The swimmer in the glide phase is seen from an underwater view in 1. The legs and arms are fully extended. The head is on the surface. In 2 the arms move apart and to the side as they reach for the catch. The hands bend at the wrist and drop slightly, turning out to the side. By 3 the catch has been made and the pull cycle has begun; 4 and 5 show the maximum force of the pull. Notice that the arms are beginning to move back in toward the body. Note the very important fact that there is no push cycle in this power phase of the armstroke. The arms are approaching recovery before passing the shoulder line. In 6 and 7 the arms are in recovery; they are bending at the elbow and the hands are returning to the chest. During recovery the swimmer maintains control while in the water, not only with the hands but with the insides of the arms; a thrust is made with the length of the arm. By 8 the arms are well into the recovery stage, moving up the chest, hands together, and arms extending beyond the head for the glide. *It is important that there be no pause between the power phase and complete recovery.*

As the power phase of the arms nears its end, the legs are starting to recover. Thus, when the power phase of the arms has been completed and the arms are entering the recovery stage, the legs can take over. In 9, 10, and 11 the body has reached the glide, arms extended, and the legs are executing their power phase kick. With the hands and arms in negative drag of recovery, the legs are providing a positive thrust forward.

The arms and hands remain extended during the kick and after the power phase of the kick; they remain in this position for the glide. This glide phase following the kick is a very important part of the breaststroke.

It is extremely important that the pull of the arms in the power phase be kept in a narrow plane. This permits a more subtle recovery of the arms and a lessening of the negative force underwater. This is the same rule that is followed for the recovery of the legs. In the breaststroke, both the arms and the legs make their recovery completely underwater and the negative force thus created must always be minimized.

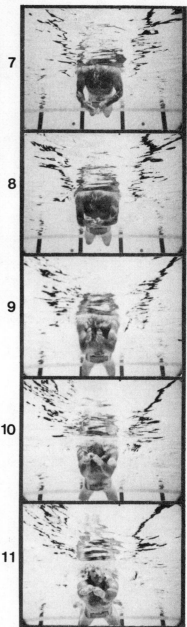

Armstroke (below water)

In the recovery phase of the armstroke, the swimmer uses the insides of his arms, as well as his hands, to keep possession of the water.

The legs and arms are fully extended for the very important glide phase of the breaststroke.

The Total Stroke

In examining the total stroke, close attention should be paid to the timing of its separate elements. This timing is the key to a successful breaststroke.

In 1 the swimmer is in the glide phase; 2 shows the arms beginning their catch while the legs are still maintaining glide position. In 3 the power phase of the arms commences. The legs are still in glide. In 4 the arms are nearing the maximum of their pull cycle in the power phase. The legs are still gliding. Photo 5 marks the end of the arms' power phase; now the legs begin their recovery. The legs have nearly recovered (6) and the arms have begun to recover and are entering their negative stage. The arms are at half-recovery in 7; the legs have completed recovery and are commencing their power phase kick (8). The hands have now reached full recovery and are extended. The legs are two-thirds of the way through their power phase kick in 9; 10 shows the completion of the kick with the arms in the glide position. By 11 armstroke and kick have been completed and the body is in glide phase.

Again, it must be emphasized that in the armstroke power phase the arms do not pull beyond the shoulder line. However, after a dive or during the turn in the breaststroke this rule is changed. This modification of the armstroke, described in "The Underwater Pull," will be demonstrated at a later stage.

Total Stroke

8

9

10

11

Total Stroke

Breathing in Stroke

In 1 the body is in the latter stage of the glide. The arms and legs are fully extended. The head is never completely below the surface of the water. A portion of the back and top of the head will always be above water. How much depends on how fast the swimmer is moving through the water. If he is moving at a rapid rate, a bow wave is created and water will seem to cover his head. But a portion of the head will always remain above the natural waterline. During the breathing phase the movement of the head should be minimized as much as possible. The eyes should be kept open.

Photo 2 shows the beginning of the catch made by the arms; the head is beginning to emerge from the water (3 and 4) — literally

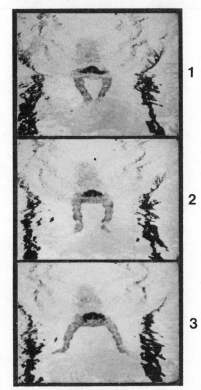

1

2

3

Breathing in Stroke

lifted out by the pull of the hands at the beginning of the armstroke power phase. Both 5 and 6 show the maximum power phase of the arms, with more than half the face now breaking through the water. In 7 the mouth is shown out of the water. The water turbulence in the bow wave shows the swimmer's blasting out of air, just as was learned in the bobbing and breathing exercises.

At this stage, a beginning swimmer is apt to thrust his shoulders back and tilt his head so that it is farther out of the water. This is not desirable since head movement should be minimized. Ideally, it is the chin that should be thrust forward; that movement alone brings the mouth into proper position for breathing. The chin is pushing forward and the head is at its highest position out of the water (8). The arms can be seen below the water at the end of their power phase. The legs (not visible) are making their catch and commencing the kick power phase. *It is now that the breath should be taken!*

By 9, the legs are in full power phase, the arms are extending for the glide, and the head is already going under (10). The head should not be turned under with the face tilting down toward the pool floor. The chin should merely be lowered and the head should remain forward. This will minimize the up-and-down movement of the body which will follow the head.

Again, it must be emphasized that the entire head is not permitted to go below the water during the stroke; a breath is taken on every power phase of the arms. This position of the head is looked at very closely in competitive swimming and the waterline on the head is judged to be above the eyes and below the hairline, as it is in the crawl.

Breathing in Stroke

Blast out all reserve air as the head is raised for a new breath.

The position of the head in relation to the natural waterline is very important in competition swimming.

The Underwater Pull

The underwater pull is executed only after a push-off and glide; a turn, push-off, and glide; or at the end of the racing dive. It is executed only once, either just before the swimmer begins the regular breaststroke (after the racing dive or push-off and glide), or before he resumes it (following the turn, push-off, and glide).

Number 1 shows the swimmer in the glide phase after a racing dive; note that his water depth is consequently greater than it would be in the glide phase during the regular breaststroke. The object here is to stay lower in the water, avoiding the surface turbulence. The head, too, is noticeably underwater, but *only* for the underwater pull!

In 2 we see the beginning of the catch for the arms. The legs remain extended. Only the power phase of the arms will be operating at this point. Both 3 and 4 show the pull cycle of the arms. In 5 and 6 the forearms drop and narrow. The upper arms move in toward the body. The entire arm has passed the shoulder line. This marks the end of the pull cycle in the underwater pull. And it begins the push cycle of the arms, a cycle that occurs *only* in the underwater pull.

The forearms push straight back to the thighs (7 and 8), joining the legs in glide. But now the arms are extended back instead of forward. Photo 9 shows the end of the pull, the hands against the thighs, the body in a streamlined contour.

This glide is maintained (as it is in the push-off, dive, and at the end of this underwater pull) until the water is felt to be slowing down around the body. But the forward momentum should never be lost. Before this happens, the recovery of the arms begins.

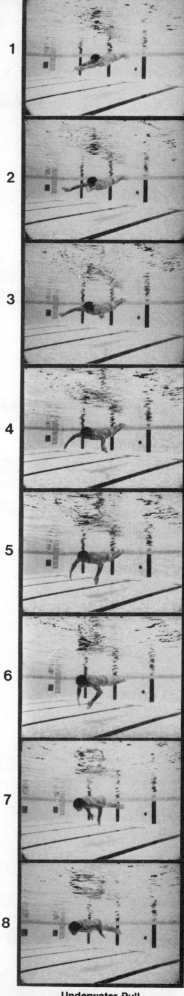

Underwater Pull

The hands are against the thighs for a streamlined contour at the end of the underwater pull glide.

The beginning of this arm recovery (10) involves the arms bending at the elbow and lifting slightly. This movement will help to keep the arms in a very narrow plane close to the body. In 11 we see the beginning of the recovery of the legs in a very subtle and narrow movement; the negative force of recovery in both arms and legs is thus held at a minimum.

In 12 the legs have recovered two-thirds of the way. The arms have reached the mid-recovery stage. Photos 13 and 14 show the beginning and maximum catch for the legs just before the power phase kick. Notice that, while the arms are almost fully extended and at the end of recovery, the legs are halfway through their power

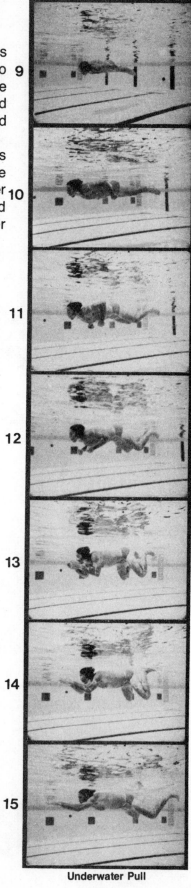

Underwater Pull

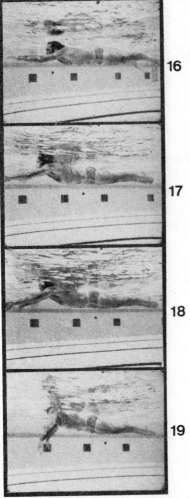

Underwater Pull

phase (15). In 16 we see the arms fully extended as the ankles are snapping back and the feet coming together in preparation for the glide. The head is already moving toward the surface; it breaks through the water as the legs go into glide (17).

The body has returned to a surface glide position, legs and arms extended. The swimmer may now proceed with the regular breaststroke, beginning with the catch of the arms (18 and 19).

Turn, Push-off, and Glide

Ideally, the approach to the wall should be made during the middle
of the glide phase with the arms extended in front.

In 1 the swimmer has made contact with the wall. Both hands
must touch the wall simultaneously; one hand can be somewhat
lower. In this case, the swimmer is turning to his right, so his right
shoulder and hand are slightly lower in the water.

Photo 2 shows the recovery of the legs; they are bending as
they normally would at the knees. In 3 the right hand has left the
wall and is assisting the body by pushing it out of the water and into
a vertical position. As the right arm extends back into the water
toward the opposite end of the pool, it brings the body around with
it. The elbow will lead the right arm into this position.

The left hand is still on the wall. The head is above water as the
body turns; at this point the breath is taken (4).

Once the body has turned, the feet are in position (from the
bending of the knee) to be planted against the wall. The head is
now turned toward the opposite end of the pool. At this stage, the
body is in the same position it would be in the turn for both the crawl
and the butterfly.

In photos 5 and 6 the left hand is seen leaving the wall and
entering the water in much the same way it does in the crawl stroke.

It is important to note that the body is reentering the water on
its side. This lateral position will cut through the water more cleanly
and with less resistance. If the body entered the water on a flatter
plane, it would encounter more resistance and would not submerge
as deeply as one would desire. Reentering the water on your side
avoids surface tension and turbulence and prevents a locking of the
shoulders.

The right arm will help take the body down into the water. As
soon as it is joined by the left arm under the water (7), the legs push
off from the wall (8), and the body goes into a glide. From the glide,
it executes the underwater pull. From the underwater pull, the
swimmer begins his regular breaststroke. For turn, push-off, and
glide underwater, see underwater pull photo sequence, 14–17.

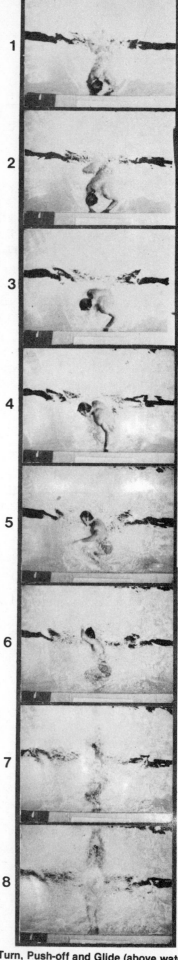

Turn, Push-off and Glide (above water)

In preparation for a turn, both hands must make contact with the wall simultaneously.

After a turn, the swimmer reenters the water on his side to reduce resistance.

THE BUTTERFLY

As was stated earlier, the push-off and glide for the butterfly is the same as that used for the crawl and the breaststroke.

The Kick

In this sequence, the kick is demonstrated with the aid of a kickboard. It can also be learned in a stationary position at the wall.

In 1 the legs are seen extended at the bottom of the kick. The legs are straight and fairly level with the surface. The toes of the feet are pointing down to the pool floor. This is the beginning of the recovery stage.

In 2 the legs begin to bend at the knee. By 3 they have reached the end of recovery with the heels leading. Note that the legs are bent to a considerable degree; the thrust will come from the knees down. Although there is some hip motion, it is not emphasized in the intermediate stage of this kick. If the swimmer is traveling slowly through the water, the thrust from the legs is needed to provide the power that will lift the body out of the water.

In 3 the legs are fully bent and the toes and feet are pointed back. The legs are now in possession of the water and they begin their power phase kick. During kick and recovery, the legs remain fairly close together.

Photo 4 shows the legs about two-thirds of the way through the power phase; they are generating a powerful thrust.

By 5 the legs have reached the end of the power phase. In 6 they are at their maximum extension and approaching recovery.

As the swimmer becomes more sophisticated in this stroke, his

58

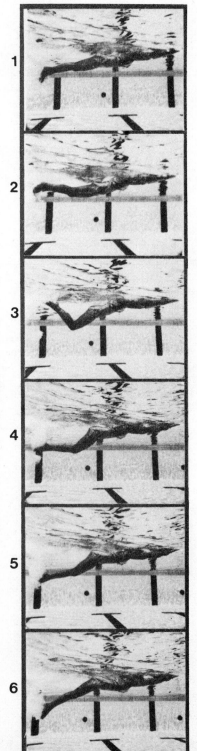

Kicking (with kickboard)

Swimmer Russell Webb demonstrates the part of the armstroke that gives the butterfly breaststroke its name.

sense of timing will improve. The use of the arms will become more pronounced while the use of the kick will be minimized.

In distance swimming, the butterfly kick is valuable at 100 yards, less valuable at 200 yards, and is used just enough to keep the hips on the water's surface. The arms, which are more efficient, take over; the blood supply to the arms is increased while it is decreased for the legs, since they are doing less work.

The use of the kickboard in this exercise will tend to exaggerate the bending of the knees during recovery and will also provide a larger thrust from the knees down.

When the armstroke is combined with the kick, the body takes on an undulating movement and the kick becomes vertically narrower, with less bending at the knee. The bulk of the forward propulsion is then provided by the arms.

Advanced Stage of the Kick

Here, in 1, the depth of the kick is not as great. The legs have reached the end of their power phase; in 2 their recovery begins. The heels are leading to the surface; they reach it in 3. The legs are parallel at all times and move together as a unit. In 4 the power phase begins, and in 5 the legs are into their downward thrust.

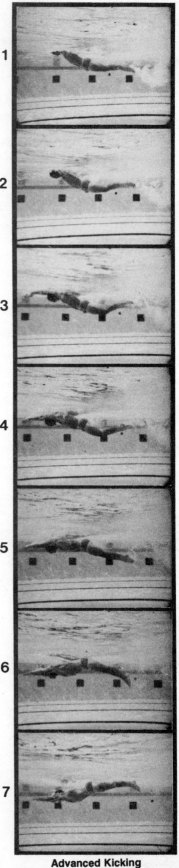

Advanced Kicking

For the butterfly kick, the legs remain together and perform simultaneously.

Notice that the knees are bending less than they did in the beginning or intermediate stage, and the legs are not entering into a deep recovery. The recovery here is a shallow one. Photo 6 illustrates the undulating movement of the body when the arms are involved. The kick is now at the bottom of the power phase. The legs begin their recovery in 7 and by 8 they have completed recovery and approach the power phase of the kick. In 9 the legs have extended to the surface; the catch is made in 10. Photo 11 marks the beginning of the power phase of the kick, shown in full in 12, 13, and 14. This involves the body from the waist down. However, most of the thrust comes from the movement of the knees to the feet. The catch for the leg power phase is made with the instep of the feet leading and extending all the way to the knees.

Advanced Kicking

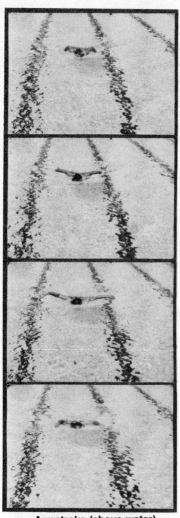

Armstroke (above water)

The Armstroke

We pick this stroke up at the end of the push cycle of the arms (1). It is very important to complete this push cycle. If the arms do not push all the way back before they swing forward, the early onset of fatigue is inevitable.

At the end of the push cycle, the elbows lead the arms out of the water for the beginning of their recovery. As they do so, the wrists must turn and bring the hands around so that the palms are facing down. This will prevent the shoulders from locking when the arms are brought around from behind to their forward position out of the water. In 2 the arms are no longer in the water. They are above the surface, making recovery in 3. Photo 4 shows their reentry into the water and the beginning of the catch, with the arms at a slight angle away from the body and the fingers entering the water first. The elbows are slightly raised.

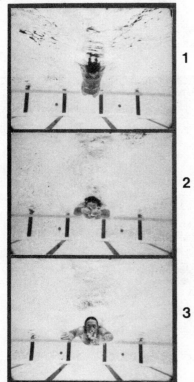

Armstroke (below water)

In the recovery phase, the palms should face downward as they break the water's surface.

The fingertips lead the arms into the catch phase.

Bent, the elbows lead the hands, palms down, out of the water.

4 The movement of the arms out of the water on recovery begins at the end of the push cycle, with the arms and hands down at the sides of the body under the water. The hands are at the thighs, having completed their push cycle. The tendency is to rotate the hands with the palms turning toward the surface. This is wrong. When the hands break through the water, the palms should be facing the surface and not turned away from it. So when the hands turn at the thighs, the palms should rotate toward the pool floor.

5 When they leave the water they will be facing the surface. The elbows should lead the hands out of the water and be slightly higher, and they remain so in the recovery phase. The hands are held in a straight line with the forearm. The elbows are slightly bent. Now the arms reach forward and, as in the crawl, they are high enough to clear an imaginary barrel floating in front — only now both arms are making that reach simultaneously.

6 The recovery of the arms in the butterfly, as in the crawl and backstroke, is not as crucial as what happens with the arms underwater during their power phase. This power phase will determine the success of your stroke.

In 1 the power phase begins. The head is down as the arms make the catch with the hands entering first. In 2 the hands are six inches or so below the surface. This catch phase appears similar to the catch phase of the breaststroke (3). In 4 the arms appear to be

7 starting a wide arc away from the body; this is the beginning of the pull cycle. At 5 the arcing out of the arms is cut short and they are at their maximum width. Now the hands pull in toward the body and the elbows follow, bending the arms. The arms are thus foreshortened to give them greater strength. As the hands approach their vertical position (6) and point down to the pool floor, the greatest thrust of the power phase is achieved; the arms, passing the shoulder line, are now moving into the push cycle. The hands come very

8 close together (7) and the push cycle is completed (8, 9, and 10), with the hands ending at the thighs in preparation for the recovery of the arms.

The stroke begins in a narrow plane, widens, and returns to a narrowing of the arms.

9

10

Armstroke (below water)

Breathing in Stroke

Photo 1 shows the beginning of the catch for the arms. As the arms begin their pull cycle in 2, the head is brought to the surface and the chin is pushed forward, as in the breaststroke. Again it should be stressed that the head is not tilted back and lifted out of the water with the shoulders.

The mouth is above the surface (3) and the swimmer is blasting out his air. The arms are nearing the end of the push cycle in the power phase. In 4 the swimmer is taking his breath. The head returns to the water (5) and the arms are beginning recovery.

In 6 the head is in the water and the arms are breaking the surface. The palms face down. At 7 the head is thrust back into the water and the hands are making the catch for the power phase of the arms. Notice the fingers go into the water first (8).

In the butterfly, it is advisable to breathe on every other arm-stroke. The body should be kept as low in the water as possible.

The Turn

In the turn for the butterfly, both hands must recover above the surface of the water and meet the wall simultaneously before making the turn. Even if the swimmer reaches the wall during his pull cycle in the power phase for the arms, he must break that cycle and reach out of the water with both arms and grab for the wall with both hands at the same time.

The turn is executed in the same manner as it is done in the breaststroke.

In the push-off and glide — which is also the same as in the breaststroke — the beginning swimmer in the butterfly will start the recovery stage of the kick once he or she is in the glide. Then the power phase of the kick is executed while the arms are still extended for the glide. This is followed by a recovery of the legs, then a power-phase kick, and now the arms move into the pull cycle of their power phase. This power phase is completed through the push cycle and the arms continue into recovery.

The timing here is critical. Once again: there are two kicks to one pull and push of the arms, and *there is a pause* between the two kicks that come one after the other before the arms move. After the arms complete this power phase, they enter recovery and the swimmer begins the total stroke.

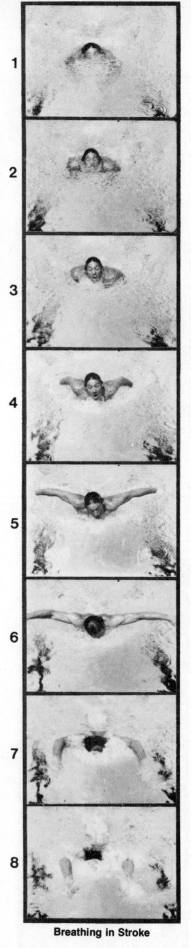

Breathing in Stroke

A breath should be taken on every *other* armstroke during the power phase of the stroke.

A breath is also taken while the head is out of the water for the turn.

The Total Stroke

In the butterfly there will be a kick and recovery of the legs during the power phase of the arms, and a kick and recovery of the legs during the recovery of the arms. The more sophisticated swimmer will enter the stroke from a push-off and glide with a kick; then a kick and pull of the arms; then a kick and arm recovery. And then he is back into the stroke.

The beginning swimmer will require a double cycle of two kicks and a pull before he enters the stroke with a recovery of the arms out of water.

The two kicks are likewise differentiated. When the arms are recovering, the kick is small. When the arms are in power phase, the kick is big. It is during this big kick that the breath is taken — but *only on every other power phase of the arm,* accompanied by its big kick.

In 1 and 2 the arms are making their catch, and the legs have completed their first kick. Photo 3 shows the catch being made and the legs entering recovery. In 4 the legs have completed recovery and are nearing the surface. In 5 the legs are in the downward thrust of the second kick and the arms are in their power phase, approaching the pull cycle. The legs are shown at the bottom of their thrust in the big kick (6) while the arms are entering the pull cycle at 7. In 8 the legs are recovering from the second kick and

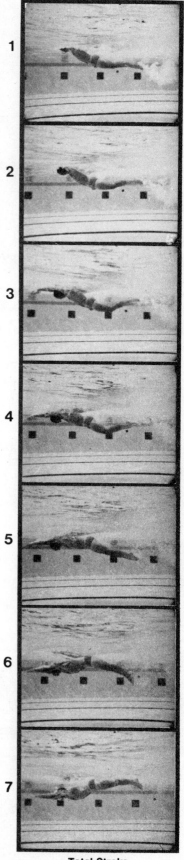

Total Stroke

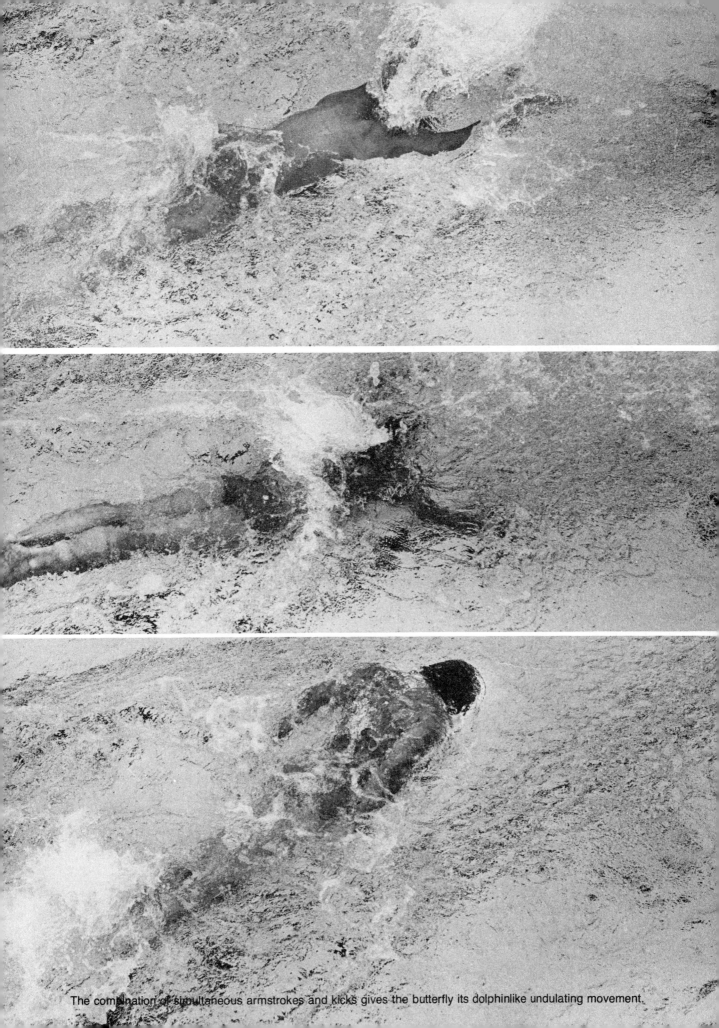

The combination of simultaneous armstrokes and kicks gives the butterfly its dolphinlike undulating movement.

have moved to the surface (9). In 10 the arms are starting to pull, and in 11 they approach the end of the pull cycle. As the arms enter the push cycle (12), the kick enters another power phase and in 13 both arms and legs come to the end of their power phases. This action is completed by 14.

Taking another look at it from the start (1, 2, and 3), we are seeing the recovery of the arms and the small kick of the legs. In 4, 5, and 6 we are seeing the power phase of the arms and the big kick.

The beginning or intermediate student of the butterfly will employ a double kick for each power phase and each recovery of the arm, and the undulating effect of the body will not be stressed until the timing of the stroke is learned. As the student becomes more sophisticated and operates with one small kick for recovery and one big kick for power phase, the undulation of the body — or its dolphinlike movement — will evolve in a natural manner.

Total Stroke

TREADING WATER

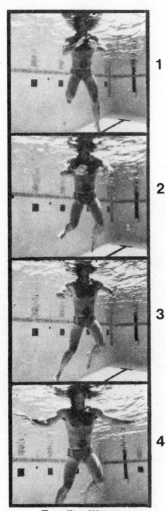

Treading Water

In 1 the hands are seen in a power phase, which is constant. They are close together. The palms are facing down. The arms are bent slightly and the elbows held out from the body. Photo 2 shows that the hands have turned out at the wrist and away from the body. As the hands push outward they also press down on the water and proceed at a diagonal. The hands do not necessarily move down in the water. Ideally they move to the side, but because the palms are angled out on a diagonal, they effectively press the water down (3).

At 4 the arms are at their full extension and the hands are rotating at the wrist (5), turning the palms in toward the body and now they begin their move back toward each other (6 and 7). In 8 the palms are leveling off and in 9 they are returning to their diagonal for the press out and down.

The arms should always be relaxed — never held straight out. The hand is always ahead of the elbow in the movement of the arm.

The legs, meanwhile, are executing a frog kick — one leg at a time — more commonly called the eggbeater kick. In 1 the left leg is extended at the end of its power phase and the right leg is bent and has recovered from its power phase. It is now at the catch and at the beginning of another power phase. As the right leg is extended in the power phase, the toes must be turned up and the foot is pointed out — the heel turned in, just as in the catch for the breast-stroke whip kick (2). Notice that as the left leg recovers, the heel is leading and the foot is extended with toes pointing. This position diminishes the negative force on recovery.

71

In treading water, the palms of the hands always face downward — but they slant *toward* each other on the approach and *away* from each other on the retreat.

In the power phase, the foot must be positioned correctly in order to capture the water beneath it.

While treading water, the body should be tilted slightly forward for extra buoyancy.

Treading Water

5

6

7

8

9

Photo 3 shows the right leg nearing the end of the power phase and the left leg extending for the recovery. In 4 the left leg is approaching its catch. In 5 the right leg is fully extended and the left leg is beginning its thrust with the toes of the foot turning out. The correct position of the foot, turned out and in possession of the water, is shown in 6. The inside of the foot is always used for this downward thrust, as well as the inside of the leg, just as in the breaststroke kick.

The body is always tilted slightly forward in the water. The legs trail behind the chest and when the legs move in their kick, they move slightly out from the body. The body should never be vertical in the water. When it is tilted forward, backward, or on its side, more of it is in the water and greater buoyancy results.

Essential to the technique of treading water is the perfection of the whip kick from the breaststroke. Of course, this kick must be relearned so that the legs are operating alternately, one leg at a time. Most of the leg movement in the kick will take place from the knee to the foot. There is little or no movement from the hip.

In survival treading water, the head is under the water, returning to the surface for the breathing phase. With the head down in the water, the arms slightly forward, and the body bent slightly at the waist, one can remain virtually motionless in the water until the head is lifted for a breath. When the head is lifted, a quick breath must be taken. The head out of water has lost its buoyancy, and its weight will push you under. So you slowly sink and slowly expel your air. But as the head returns to the water, so does your buoyancy and you start to rise once again to the surface. This buoyancy will carry you to beyond the surface where you can get another breath of air and repeat the cycle. So a combination of controlled breathing and perpetual motion can support a swimmer effortlessly in the water until he or she falls asleep, starves, or freezes to death.

SUPPLEMENTAL EXERCISES

With the Inner Tube

This small inflatable inner tube can be bought at a sporting goods store. Or it can be found in a garden tools supply shop since it is exactly the size of an inner tube from a power-mower tire.

It is used to restrain the legs from executing a kick, and it isolates the arms so that their function can be exercised. Its best feature is that it puts the body in a correct position in the water — parallel to the surface.

It will also create a tremendous amount of drag, forcing the arms to overcompensate and to function as if they were training with weights.

One foot is placed through the hole from the topside. The other foot passes through the hole from the underside. When the legs are straightened out, the tire twists into a kind of pretzel shape. Now, once you're in the water, the tire can't slip from your ankles and float away.

This device will supplement out-of-the water calisthenics, and workouts with counter-weights in the gym, both designed to strengthen the arms.

The best armstroke to use with the inner tube is the freestyle or crawl. If you are perfecting one of the other strokes, it should be added to your workout. This use of the inner tube should comprise about one-third of your training time.

With the Hand Paddles

The use of the paddles is designed primarily for learning how to take possession of the water with the hands. In order to do this effectively, the hand must be taught to operate constantly as near to 90 degrees to the surface as possible during the power phase of the arms.

Coach Horn and Russell Webb place a small inner tube exerciser on the legs of swimmer Diana Dann.

While restricting the kick, the inner tube's buoyancy keeps the swimmer's body parallel to the surface.

Working with hand paddles quickly points out and corrects improper hand positioning . . .

. . . especially when used in conjunction with the inner tube.

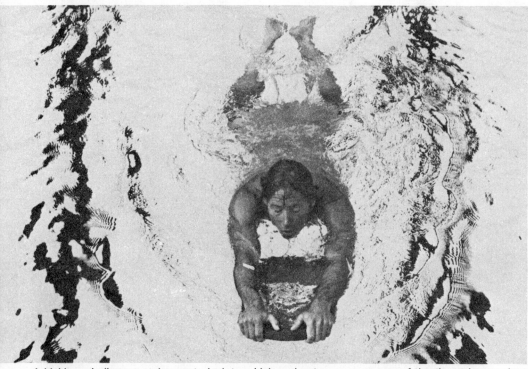

A kickboard allows a swimmer to isolate a kick and get some measure of the thrust he receives.

If the hand is angled or tilted during any part of the power phase, it is not noticed by the hand alone as it moves through the water. But when the hand is wearing a plastic paddle, the hand and paddle will slide on the water if the correct angle is not achieved.

The paddle moving through the water will encounter more resistance than the hand. Attached to the hand, it provides a kind of weight-training in the water for the arms.

This paddle can be bought at a sporting goods store. Some are made so that they are contoured for the hand to slip in on one side. Others merely have elastic fasteners that slip over the back of the hand.

With the Kickboard

The use of the kickboard isolates the legs and permits movement through the water while learning and perfecting a kick. This gives the swimmer a more accurate feeling for the kick in the water than he would get when practicing the kick from the wall. He or she certainly gets a better idea of the kind of propulsion that results from the kick.

The kickboard should be held between halfway and two-thirds of the way up, grasping it so that the thumb is on the topside and the fingers on the underside. The head should be kept low. This is also a good way to practice breath control.

With the head held down the kick comes closer to the surface. With the head held up, the hips and legs will drop. When you become more proficient in kicking, you can afford the luxury of keeping your head up at all times during this exercise.

This kickboard can be bought at any sporting goods store. It is called "The Water Wonder." Rounded at one end — the end pointing away from the body — and squared off at the other, it is held between your arms.

Grasp the kickboard firmly and hold it out in front of you at arms' length.

The kickboard can be used in practicing and perfecting the backstroke kick as well as all others.

THE RACING DIVE

The Racing Dive

This is the standing, fast dive from the edge of the pool. It is used in collegiate and AAU (Amateur Athletic Union) competition.

The swimmer stands at the edge of the pool. The toes are hooked over the side of the pool wall, or over the edge of the starting block.

In international swimming competition, the swimmer stands one step behind the edge of the pool.

In 1 the swimmer stands in readiness, arms at his side, toes hooked over the edge, head up. He concentrates on the race and listens for the starter.

At the command, "Take your mark!" (2), the arms move forward. In 3 the head leans forward and the hands rise. The hands are out in front in 4 and the upper body is dropping forward with the knees slightly bent. Photo 5 shows the counterbalanced position with the hands extended in front, the head looking forward. The arms are held at about a 45-degree angle. The eyes focus on the opposite end of the pool. In 6 the back is almost level with the water and the head and shoulders are slightly above the hips. As the starting gun fires, the head goes down (7) and the hands move slightly forward and out in a small, circular motion. Then the arms

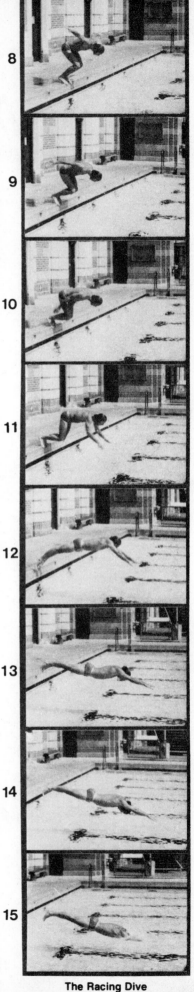

swing back toward the hips (8) and the hands are above the hips in 9. In 10 the arms move back toward the hips and the drive is now transferred to the front, throwing the body off balance and into a falling motion toward the water. The thrust now starts from the legs. The timing of the drive of the arms and the thrust of the legs is extremely important. As the drive of the arms transfers from a backward swing into a forward motion at the hip, the legs begin their thrust.

In 11 the legs are at the maximum of their thrust and the head is starting to come up. The complete extension of the legs is shown in 12. The hands do not rise to nor exceed the level of the shoulders, but are angled just below the shoulder line. Photo 13 shows the body in full extension, off the wall and in the air. The diver is almost parallel to the surface of the water with the head and shoulders slightly lower than the feet.

Between 13 and 14, the head is dropping back down to parallel the arms, and now the body is in full extension, with the hands together, legs extended and toes pointed. At 15 the head is down between the arms, making the shoulders as narrow as possible and a clean entry into the water is made, fingers first.

If the hands or head are too high, the body will land flat on the surface, or worse, feet first, for a very mushy entry.

The purpose of the proper angle in this dive is to make a clean opening hole with the hands and let the rest of the body follow in after. The angle should not be too oblique or the dive will be too deep. For a racing start, the dive should be clean, swift and shallow in the water.

The Racing Dive

Moments after the starting gun, the arms are back and the diver falls toward the water.

The head must be down between the arms for a clean, finger-first entry.

THE RECREATIONAL DIVE

In photo 1 the swimmer is shown with toes hooked over the edge of the pool wall. The hands move forward slightly in 2. By 3 the arms are following, rising and moving forward, and 4 shows the body off balance. The arms swing back in a wider arc for this dive (5). They go higher and further back. In 6 the body is falling forward, while 7 marks the beginning of the power phase for the arms and legs which work together in 8 for maximum thrust, reached in 9.

By 10 the body is ready to leave the wall, and in 11 the head is dropping between the arms which are taking on a much steeper angle than we saw in the racing dive. This will be a deeper, slower

The Recreational Dive

The Recreational Dive

dive. To achieve this angle the hands should stop their descent toward the water when they reach a level with the edge at the opposite end of the pool. The eye must spot this just before the head drops fully between the arms as in 12. The body is now following the head and arms toward the surface of the water. The fingers break the water in 13.

Ideally, the motion of the body is up, over and down. It is going over that imaginary barrel again, but a larger barrel this time and in the mid-air photo, 11, the body is seen in a slight "U" shape.

WATER SAFETY

Although pool swimming is considered safe (compared to swimming in lakes, with their sudden holes and clumps of weeds, and ocean bathing, where rip tides may drag the swimmer away from the shore), drownings still occur. Sometimes the cause can be traced to an unforeseen health problem or an accident that incapacitates a swimmer or causes him to lose consciousness. But all too often, drownings in pools and elsewhere occur because people violate or ignore safety practices. Here are ten simple rules which should be followed for water safety:

1. Learn to swim well enough to survive in an emergency.
2. Swim with a buddy who has the ability to help when necessary.
3. Swim only in supervised areas.
4. Know your limitations and do not overestimate your ability.
5. Stay out of the water when overheated, overtired and immediately after eating.
6. Dive only in known water of sufficient depth.
7. Avoid long periods of immersion and overexposure to the sun.
8. Take instruction under qualified instructors before participating in aquatic sports.
9. Follow rules set up for the particular pool, beach, or waterfront where you are swimming.
10. Call for help only when you really need it.

Water safety also means reacting positively to swimming emergencies. In this regard, the three basic rules are:

1. Do not panic.
2. Think.
3. Save your strength.

One of the difficulties that sometimes causes unsure swimmers to panic is getting a cramp. Most cramps experienced in the water are the kind that affect fingers, toes, arms, or legs. They are usually caused by muscle fatigue or overexertion. Although painful, cramps are not incapacitating and are of little danger to the swimmer if he keeps his head. Changing the swimming stroke and relaxing will often bring relief. If the cramp continues, rubbing and kneading the affected part while holding on to the pool wall or practicing the survival treading-water technique if away from the pool wall may help. Most important, however, is the stretching of the affected muscle. For example, a cramp in the calf of the leg, which may be caused by the continued arching or pointing of the foot, can be worked out best by flexing the ankle and forcing the toes upward toward the kneecap, a direction opposite to the pointing foot, thus stretching the calf muscle. If this stretching process and change of stroke is initiated as soon as a swimmer feels a distinct twinge or warning sign, the cramp may be avoided or reduced.

Stomach cramps, which have been attributed to overexertion too soon after eating, are not common but they do occur. This kind of cramp, more accurately called an abdominal cramp, need not be as serious as formerly believed. If the swimmer will relax, change his body position, and stretch out, his natural buoyancy should keep him afloat until the cramp subsides. In order to do this, the swimmer must not panic but must recognize the cramp for what it is — a difficulty, not impending disaster — and follow the procedures that will bring relief and safety.

Other hazards for nonpool swimmers are river currents, undertows, and weeds. When caught in a current, a swimmer should not attempt to buck or fight it. Instead he should swim directly *across* the current. Though this may bring the swimmer out further downstream, it will enable him to reach safety without becoming exhausted.

Swimmers encountering undertows and rip tides become alarmed when they find themselves being dragged away from the shore. But, again, the victim should not panic or struggle against the current, as this would cause him to quickly expend his strength. He should swim parallel to the shoreline *across* the current and, once he is free of it, swim to shore.

When caught in weeds, it is important that the swimmer not thrash around or make quick, vigorous movements, since this only tends to entangle the victim still further. Slow, careful arm movements with just a gentle waving action of the legs will allow the swimmer to work his way loose.

COMPETITIVE SWIMMING

For those of you who have had your appetite whetted by this book for swimming as a sport rather than as simple recreation, here are some facts about competitive swimming.

The four basic strokes covered in this book — crawl, backstroke, breaststroke, and butterfly — are the strokes performed in competitive swimming. The freestyle stroke you hear about in competitive swimming is simply another term for the crawl. The butterfly is a relatively new stroke which evolved from the breaststroke several years ago.

At the collegiate level, the distances in the backstroke, breaststroke, and butterfly are limited to 100 and 200 yards. In the freestyle or crawl events, the distances range from 50 yards to 100, 200, 500, 1000, and 1650 yards. The latter is called the *swimming mile*.

There is also a competitive swimming event called the *individual medley*. To compete in this event, an individual swimmer must perform all four of the basic strokes in turn. First the butterfly, then the backstroke, following that with the breaststroke and ending with the freestyle or crawl. The strokes are always done in that order, and each stroke is swum an equal distance. For example, in a 200-yard individual medley, 50 yards is devoted to each stroke, while in a 400-yard medley, each of the four strokes is performed for 100 yards.

Another swimming competition is the relay. This is team swimming. In the freestyle relay, each of the four swimmers on a team will swim freestyle one-quarter of the relay distance. In a 400-yard relay each entry swims 100 yards, while in an 800-yard relay each swimmer undertakes a 200-yard distance. In a medley relay, the first swimmer does the backstroke, the second swimmer does the breaststroke, the third swimmer follows with the butterfly, and the fourth swimmer finishes up the event with the freestyle. Medley relays are usually 400 yards long with each swimmer doing 100 yards in his stroke.

This is the gamut of swimming events — even at the Olympics. Of course, at the Olympics, distances are measured in meters rather than our yards. The Olympic pools are 50 meters (54.68 yards) in length.

In a dual collegiate meet, three swimmers from each of the two teams are allowed to swim in each event. Although six swimmers may be in the pool during that event, only two out of the three entries from each school will count in the scoring. Even if the third swimmer from a team swims faster than the fastest swimmer of the opposing team, he or she cannot place third. That honor goes to the speediest member on the competing team.

Many countries send swimmers to compete in the Olympic Games, but the countries themselves are not competing. The swimmers compete against each other as individuals. As many as eight swimmers may compete in the preliminaries of each event. The number of swimmers may vary in these matches, as the swimmers are primarily competing against the clock. In the final matches, only the eight top swimmers who qualify on a time basis will compete in each event for the coveted Olympic medals.

In the United States, swimming is a year-round sport. Collegiate and inter-collegiate (high school) teams hold their meets between Thanksgiving and the latter part of April. All events are held in 25-yard pools. In collegiate competition, a student's scholastic record determines his or her eligibility for participation in meets. Also during the winter, short-course meets sanctioned by the Amateur Athletic Union are held throughout the country. Anyone with an AAU card who submits the minimum qualifying time established for an AAU event may enter in the competition. Junior meets, however, are limited by age levels. A particular event may be open only to participants seventeen years and under, ten years and under, and so on. In the summer months the swimming season is termed *long course* and the events are usually held outdoors. There are dozens of AAU meets throughout the country every week of the year.

An AAU card, verifying your amateur status, can be obtained at your local AAU office for a small registration fee (the amount may vary slightly from one part of the country to another). Your AAU card and your ability to meet the qualifying time posted for the event you wish to enter are all you need to enter competition. An AAU swimming rulebook (which governs AAU meet events) and guides on swimming and on other amateur athletic sports — including basketball, judo, boxing, and track — are available from the Amateur Athletic Union.

AMATEUR ATHLETIC UNION OFFICIAL SWIMMING RULES

Portions reprinted from *1974 Official Rules for Competitive Swimming,* copyright 1974 by the Amateur Athletic Union of the United States, Inc.

All competitive swimming events held under Amateur Athletic Union sanction shall be conducted in accordance with rules which are designed to protect the swimmer, provide fair and equitable conditions of competition, and promote uniformity in the sport so that no swimmer shall obtain an unfair advantage over another.

CLASSES OF COMPETITION

COMPETITIVE CLASSIFICATIONS — Swimming shall be conducted under the following classifications, and participation is open to athletes from any country subject to further pertinent regulations in these rules and elsewhere.

1. *Senior* — All registered swimmers are eligible for the Senior Class.

2. *Junior* — All registered swimmers 18 years of age and younger are eligible for the Junior Class subject to certain restrictions.

3. *Age Group-Junior Olympic* — Age Group – Junior Olympic Swimming is for swimmers 17 years of age and under.

4. *Masters* — Masters Swimming is for swimmers 25 years of age and older.

RULES FOR SWIMMING THE STROKES

BREASTSTROKE

1. *Start* — The forward start shall be used.

2. *Stroke* — The body shall be kept perfectly on the breast, and both shoulders shall be in line with the water surface from the beginning of the first armstroke after the start and after each turn. All movements of the arms shall be simultaneous and in the same horizontal plane without alternating movement. The hands shall be pushed forward together from the breast, and shall be brought back on or under the surface of the water. A part of the head shall always be above the general water level (the surface in a calm state), except that after the start and after each turn, the swimmer may take one arm stroke and one leg kick while wholly submerged. The instant the hands leave the extended position, a new stroke shall have been started. A wave passing over the head does not constitute a violation.

3. *Kick* — All movements of the legs shall be simultaneous and in the same horizontal plane without alternating movement. The feet must be turned outwards in the backward movement. A butterfly kick is not permitted. Breaking the surface with the feet shall not merit disqualification unless caused by movement of the legs in a vertical plane.

4. *Turns and Finish* — When touching the end of the pool or course at the turns or on finishing a race, the touch shall be made with both hands simultaneously at the same level, either at, above, or below the water level. The shoulders shall be in line with the water surface.

   Note: Either complete or incomplete movement of the arms or legs from the starting position shall be considered as one complete stroke or kick.

BUTTERFLY STROKE

1. *Start* — The forward start shall be used. After the start and turns a swimmer is permitted one or more leg kicks but only one arm pull under water, which must bring him to the surface.

2. *Stroke* — Both arms must be brought forward together over the water and brought backward simultaneously. The body must be kept perfectly on the breast and both shoulders in the horizontal plane from the beginning of the first armstroke after the start and after each turn.

3. *Kick* — All up-and-down movements of the legs and feet must be simultaneous. The position of the legs and feet shall not alternate in relation to each other. The use of the scissor or breaststroke kicking movement is not permitted.

4. *Turns and Finish* — When touching the end of the pool or course at the turns or on finishing a race, the touch shall be made with both hands simultaneously on the same level while the body is on the breast. The shoulders shall be in a horizontal position in line with the surface of the water. A legal touch may be made above or below the surface of the water.

BACKSTROKE

1. *Start* — The swimmers shall line up in the water, facing the starting end, with both hands resting either on the end or rail of the pool or on any part of the starting platform or block, or on the starting grips.

    a. Short Course — The feet may be placed in any position on the end of the pool and the swimmer may assume any desired starting position which does not remove his feet completely from the water nor his feet from contact with the end of the pool nor his hands from the starting grips, pool edge, or starting block.

    b. Long Course — It shall be the starter's duty to see that the swimmer's feet, including the toes, shall be under the surface of the water and that no swimmer is standing in or on the gutter or curling his toes over the lip of the gutter.

2. *Stroke* — The swimmer shall push off on his back and continue swimming on his back throughout the race.

3. *Turns* — The swimmer's head, foremost hand, or arm must touch the end of the course, but the shoulders must not turn over beyond the vertical before the touch is made. It is permissible to turn the shoulders over beyond the vertical after the touch in executing the turn but the swimmer must have returned to a position on the back before the feet have left the wall.

4. *Finish* — Any swimmer shall have finished the race when any part of his person touches the solid wall at the end of the pool.

FREESTYLE

1. *Start* — The forward start shall be used.

2. *Stroke* — Freestyle means that in an event so designated the swimmer may swim any style; except that in a medley relay or individual medley event, freestyle means any style other than butterfly, breaststroke, or backstroke.

3. *Turns* — In freestyle competition the hand touch is not required at the turn; it is sufficient if any part of the swimmer touches the solid wall at the end of the pool or course.

INDIVIDUAL MEDLEY — The swimmer shall swim the prescribed distance in the following order: the first one-fourth, butterfly; the second one-fourth, backstroke; the third one-fourth, breaststroke; and the last one-fourth, freestyle. Rules pertaining to each stroke used shall govern where applicable.

RELAYS

1. *Freestyle Relay* — Four swimmers on each team, each to swim one-fourth of the prescribed distance using any desired stroke(s).

2. *Medley Relay* — Four swimmers on each team, each to swim one-fourth of the prescribed distance continuously in the following order: first, backstroke; second, breaststroke; third, butterfly; and fourth, freestyle. Rules pertaining to each stroke used shall govern where applicable.

3. *Rules Pertaining to Relay Races:*
    a. No swimmer shall swim more than one leg in any relay event.
    b. Relay teams may not compete unattached and must in all cases be composed of registered members of the same club, school or-organization.
    c. In relay races a swimmer other than the first swimmer shall not start until his teammate shall have concluded his leg.
    d. Any relay team member and his relay team shall be disqualified from a race if a team member other than the swimmer designated to swim that leg shall jump into or enter the pool in the area where the race is being conducted before all swimmers of all teams have finished the race.
    e. In relay races the team of a swimmer whose feet have lost touch with the starting platform (ground or deck) before his preceding teammate touches the wall shall be disqualified.

FINISH RULES FOR ALL STROKES:

1. In all swimming races each swimmer shall have finished his race when he has covered the prescribed distance and any part of his person touches the solid wall at the end of the pool or course, except that:
   a. In the breaststroke and the butterfly, the swimmer must comply with the finish requirements for those strokes as defined under the rules for each stroke, and:
   b. If completely automatic officiating equipment is used, each swimmer must touch the touch-plate or pad in his lane at the end of pool or course to have finished his race.

GLOSSARY
Swimming Words and Terms

Across-the-Board Place Judges — two place judges, one on each side of the finish line, who will record the order of finish by lane. The independent decisions of these two judges may be used for balloting.

Appreciable — sufficient in extent to be recognized.

Association — a recognized subsidiary member of the National AAU.

Body — the torso, including shoulders and hips.

Calm State or Surface — normal level surface without turbulence.

Competitive Swimming — the act of competing for time or place against time or other swimmers.

Consolation — (finals) competition for the fastest of those who failed to qualify for the finals.

Course — designated distance over which the competition is conducted:
   Long course — 50 or 55 yards, 50 meters.
   Short course — 20 or 25 yards, 25 meters.

Draw — random selection by chance.

Event — any race or series of races in a given stroke or distance.

Final — any single race which determines final places and times in an event.

Finalist — one who swims in a final race.

Finals — the concluding session of the meet in which the Final Race of each event is swum.

Heat — a division of an event in which there are too many swimmers to compete at one time.

Horizontal — parallel to the level surface of the water.

Lane — the specific area in which the swimmer is assigned to swim, i.e., lane one, lane two, etc.

Lane Line — continuous floating markers attached to a line stretched from the starting end to the turning end for the purpose of separating each lane.

Lane Markings — the guide lines on the bottom of the pool and in the center of the lanes running from the starting end to the turning end.

Leg — (relay) the part of a relay event that is swum by a single team member.

Length — extent of the course from end to end.

Marks — (take your) starting position.

May — permissive, not mandatory.

Meet — a series of events held in one program and in the following categories:
    Closed — for members of one organization or one AAU Association.
    Open — for senior swimmers.
    Age Group/Junior Olympic — for any or all age groups.
    Junior — 18 and under.
    Masters — for masters swimmers (age 25 and over)
    Invitational — for those swimmers and clubs invited by the meet manager.
    Dual — between two teams.
    Or any combination of the above.

Pool — the physical facility in which the competition is actually conducted.

Preliminary — session of the meet in which the heats are held.

Propulsive — having power to propel.

Race — any single swimming competition, i.e., preliminary, final, timed final.

Registered — enrolled as an amateur athlete in one of the associations of the AAU.

Scissor — use of the top of the instep of one foot and the bottom of the other foot in the propulsive part of the kick.

Scratch — (from an event) withdraw an entry from competition.

Seed — distribute the swimmers among the required number of heats and/or lanes, according to their submitted or preliminary times.

Shall — mandatory.

Simultaneously — at the same time.

Solid Wall — the end of the pool including the vertical end of the pool and the front of the starting block or platform.

Split Time — the time taken at an intermediate distance.

Still Water — water contained within four walls or landlocked which has no perceptible current or movement other than that caused by wind or by other swimmers. (Circulatory systems should be off during competition.)

Submitted Times — those filed with an entry, as having been previously achieved.

Time Standard — the Time Standard for any event in a meet is the cut-off time for that event.

Timed Finals — competition in which only heats are swum and final placings are determined by the times performed in the heats.

Unattached — not representing a dues-paying member club or organization of the AAU.

Vertical — at a right angle to the normal water level.

The complete AAU *Official Rules for Competitive Swimming* is available for purchase from the AAU. Send a check or money order in the amount of $2.00 for each copy wanted to Amateur Athletic Union of the United States, 3400 West 86th Street, Indianapolis, Indiana 46268.

ABOUT COACH HORN

Named Coach of the Year for 1973 by the Collegiate Swimming Coaches Association, Bob Horn became UCLA's head swimming and water polo coach in 1963. Under his guidance the UCLA water polo team is now the number one team in the nation, and the swimming team is in fifth position as determined by the NCAA.

Horn trained the members of the U.S. Olympic team in 1964, 1968, and 1972. Six of the eleven members of the 1972 U.S. water polo team were his swimmers, and they came home with the first medal awarded to an American team that year.

Horn competed in the 1955 Pan-American Games in Mexico City and was on the U.S. Olympic teams in 1956 and 1960.

His great interest in young people accounts for his devoting his summers to the operation of the Flaming Gorge Boys and Girls Camp in Utah. For ten weeks every summer, Horn, with the help of his wife and two sons, and his partner, UCLA baseball coach Art Reichle, introduce some eighty youngsters to the excitement and adventure of outdoor living.

Coach Bob Horn

ABOUT THE SWIMMERS

DIANA DANN is an aquatics instructor at UCLA where she received her BA degree in physical education. She has been teaching beginning swimming, intermediate swimming, and skin diving, and she is continuing with her graduate studies. Her active participation in swimming sports began in junior high school and continues to this day. Her home is in Garden Grove, California.

RUSSELL WEBB began his competitive swimming in high school and continued with it at UCLA. He broke the national high school record in the 100-yard breaststroke and held that record for two years. At UCLA he broke the NCAA 100-yard breaststroke record. He set the national 400-yard medley relay record and held it for three years. He placed in the top four in the 100-meter breaststroke for three years running, taking second place for two years and fourth the third. He placed in the 200-yard breaststroke — eleventh his first year and fifth his second and third years. He went to the 1967 Pan-American Games and placed first and won the gold medal in the 400-meter medley relay. He won the silver medal in the 100-meter breaststroke. Since then he has been to the 1968 Olympic Games and the 1972 Games in water polo in which the United States won the bronze medal. He is now a graduate student at UCLA and plans a career in dentistry.

Diana Dann

Russell Webb